BURNFORT, LAS VEGAS

Other books by Martina Evans

Martina Evans

Burnfort, Las Vegas

ANVIL PRESS POETRY

Published in 2014
by Anvil Press Poetry Ltd
Neptune House   70 Royal Hill   London   SE10 8RF
www.anvilpresspoetry.com

Copyright © Martina Evans 2014

This book is published with financial assistance
from Arts Council England

Designed and set in Monotype Bembo by Anvil
Printed and bound in Great Britain
by Hobbs the Printers Ltd

ISBN 978 0 85646 457 7

A catalogue record for this book
is available from the British Library

to Joey Bryniarska

Perhaps it is only in childhood that books have any deep influence on our lives . . . but in childhood all books are books of divination, telling us about the future, and like the fortune-teller who sees a long journey in the cards or death by water they influence the future.

GRAHAM GREENE

ACKNOWLEDGEMENTS

Thanks to the editors of these publications in which poems have appeared: *Ambit*, *The Good Times* (Santa Cruz), KUSP Radio California, *The Lampeter Review* (Wales), *The Moth*, *New Letters* (U.S.), *New Planet Cabaret* (New Island Books), The Ofi Press (Mexico), *Oxford Magazine*, *Poetry Ireland Review*, Rack Press, *The Rialto*, *Riddlefence* (Canada), *Set Down* (Yew Tree Press); and the websites of the Belgian shoe museum, *Shoes Or No Shoes?* (www.shoesornoshoes.com) and of TEDxOxford (http://tedxoxford.co.uk).

Contents

Burnfort, Las Vegas

for Martin Westwood

We move the Sacred Heart lamp
closer to Elvis's face now in the month
of June. I think that those
billboards of Vegas
could be the Major cigarette sign
or the Double Diamond Works Wonders
in the lounge window round '75
or the BP pump shining
in the blue Burnfort evening,
the wood pigeons cooing
as the men come down
from the mountain and fill their vans
with petrol – a violet cloud
with a tantalizing smell and someone
says Burnfort is like New York
to those mountainy men the way
it is all built up with a school
and a church and a post office and us
city slickers running the pub,
shop and petrol pumps
and I believe it is true,
that we are like that to them –
there were stranger things then
to believe in, only now I think
it was more like Vegas, all those
signs, the games of forty-five
and my Elvis tape playing.
A few months ago
the novelty mug frightened us all

by spontaneously bursting
into *Viva Las Vegas* and I took that
as a sign, did what any
Catholic would do – put up a shrine.

My Darling Clementine

I never fail to see Daddy's hands
every time I watch *My Darling Clementine*
and this is often, as I love that film.
It's the point where Wyatt and Doc
might fight – first there's the whiskey
that Doc Holliday sends shooting down
the shining bar counter with the back
of his hand, followed by
a forty-five sliding up
from Brother Morg and sent sliding
down again before Doc and Wyatt
make their peace over champagne
and the whole room breathes
as men move back to the bar,
the conductor clicks his fingers
and the Mexican band starts to play.
I think of the story of Daddy suddenly angry
one night he had enough
and refused to be pacified with a drink
which he sent flying down
the Formica like Doc
with the back of his hand and that was
a funny anecdote to be told afterwards,
the dramatic gesture so unlike him
and I think of his swollen crooked fingers
and how he was almost always powerless.
I am sure no one was afraid for his life – if there
was a band, no way had it stopped playing
and the cowboys were drinking
steadily at the counter.

Daddy was more like Mack standing behind the bar
when Fonda asks, *Have you ever been in love?*
The small deferential bald head answers
subversively
No, I've been bartender all my life.

Gazebo

Gazebo was the word my mother
used to describe a mad exhibitionist
or a *queer hawk*. For example,
so-and-so *was going around like a
right gazebo*. Naturally I imagined
a gazebo had legs and travelled, so
I was surprised to see my first one
on an English village green, going
nowhere, the wedding couple
toasting each other under its rippling
blue and white canopy as cricket bats
smacked slowly in the heat. My mother
grew up near landed gentry
and the gazebos hidden in their walled gardens
must have entered her language
like escaped seeds,
growing into wild tramps
that straggled along the Rathkeale road,
on strange, overblown feet.

Save Us

A thin nicotine man
legs crossed showing grey socks
sits at the end of the yellow
Formica table. I'm guessing
it's 1966: slim dark suit, narrow mustard tie,
white shirt, rubbing his hands.
My mother stands over him,
he's being made to drink
black coffee, the standard drunkard's
cure. His quiff bobs over his ham
and mustard sandwich. He's not
going to be served any more drink
and he's been removed from his bad
card-playing friends round the fire, every second
phrase from my mother is – *and go home like*
a good little boy. What about her own
little boys? Her ten children trapped
in a mushroom cloud of jealousy
over love spread too thin?
My brother roars *People want to*
fucking come in here and have a drink
in peace and not listen to your fucking
sermons when she sends Jimmy the singing
toy-and-sweet traveller on his way
like a good little boy. The following day
Jimmy is in the shop clasping
my mother's hand – his gift, a bright red two-foot
statue of Our Blessed Saviour is passed
over the black wooden counter with fantastic
ease and just about as much

alcoholic sentimentality as any of us
can stand. My brother, sickened to his quick
and smoking deep, stands a mile from the house
plotting under the dripping trees.

Daddy and Mae West

*for my brother Richard Cotter, in memory of our father
Richard Cotter 1902–1988*

Come up and see me some time, you said, patting the yellow
Formica with swollen crooked hands, the morning Mae
died and Mammy said there was more to you than met
the eye, half laughing and half annoyed too, as if Mae
might have some claim on you. You were old enough to
be my grandfather and that wasn't always easy when you
were referred to as such and the truth is you didn't
believe in washing much maybe you were saving water
for you were as pathologically tight as a concentration
camp survivor, knotted laces, rusty nails, Old Moore's
Almanacs, the salvage fashion was waiting for you. Every
now and then there was a clean sweep and scrub and you
were bereft as I am now, reading my brother's email
about the farm in the forties. You sang but rarely to an
audience, I remember *Fill Up Once More* and *Glorio,
Glorio, to the bold Fenian Men* but I was a child caught up
in days of wishing, why wouldn't you wash? My brother
says that your favourite was *Felons of Our Land* and he
heard you sing *The Four Leaf Shamrock* at Yellowtown,
your tenor playing against a thick rapt silence. You'd
gone there to have a farm implement fixed. That word. I
hear you now frustrated in the seventies, asking had any
of us seen your *implement*. You used old expressions like
By Jove and called bowls *vessels*. But my brother saw you
dancing – you. *Traditional ballroom dancing* my brother
writes and *he did the Russian Sailor dance, kicking his legs
while down on his haunches.* Come up and see me some
time, I want to say. Come dancing.

Ghost Story

for Annemarie and Jim

She came home young from America round 1910 with
TB and a suitcase of fierce elegant American clothes. She
might have been a maid, I suppose, but whoever she'd
been with anyway, she'd been well got. Someone had
provided for her death. And while she was waiting to die,
she used to go for walks with a big black dog. No, I don't
know what kind of dog he was. He was big and black,
that's all I know, the two of them standing beside the
Shannon Estuary looking into the water. Then she died
of course and they buried her, and that night, weren't the
family woken up by the knocking on the window and
howling like the worst soul out of the blackest section of
hell? They could have lain in their beds all night, giving
in to themselves but their father was a rational man. He
told them get up. *Get up*, he said, *and I'll teach you some-
thing* and there was the reason below in front of them –
the bedroom window open to air the room from the
smell of the dead and the sash cord, loose in the wind,
knocking against the glass. People have this idea of ghosts
but isn't there a reason for everything? The howling?
Sure, that was only the old dog, gone demented on her
bed, turning round and round on top of the sheets and
of course, they had to shoot him too, after.

Low Key

You'd always know people who never had anything, with the blowing out of them. You'd never hear the real gentry at that. Oh no, everything would be low key. No blowing. But everything good. Their clothes might be old but they were always good. Buy good and you'll save money in the long run. A quality material, like a good tweed, it never wears out. I remember Miss Finton in a herringbone coat, I saw her in the draper's with a piece of silk held between her fingers. I think she replaced the lining twice, there's nothing wrong with thrift, it's people who never had anything throw everything away. Of course always have good gloves and shoes. Never without a pair of gloves, no matter what. Put the money into the shoes. When I see those ones going round in those scuffed white shoes – God, it looks very low, very cheap. And important to take care of the shoes too, polishing them the night before. Uncle Peter used saddle soap years ago, there was a lovely smell off it, a smell of quality. And always put the shoe-tree inside to hold the shape and don't have them thrown in a pile. And anyone who ever worked for the gentry became like them, close-mouthed. You wouldn't hear any old talk out of them. I remember one time old Liza Lawson came down with Tomeen, he must have been only two or three but he learned to talk very young. He used to be sitting up in the pram, like an old man holding conversations with people. Liza had taken him up to Lord Beddington's, wasn't she a maid there for the most of twenty-five years? And very well got by them too, they had great time for her and she even walked like them, so straight, you'd turn in the street to look at her but Tomeen must have seen something above at the Manor. Sure I don't know what he saw. Lord Beddington and the wife they didn't get on. Well, Liza was coming out in a sweat, as I said, anyone who ever worked for them became like them. Very close-mouthed. Loyal to the bone. She had to start waltzing Tomeen around the kitchen and singing over whatever he was trying to say. Tomeen must have seen Lord Beddington hitting, sure I don't know what happened only Liza was singing and going *wooh* up in the air with Tomeen and his hair flying straight up with the force and God, aren't I telling you, I couldn't hear what he was saying? I couldn't hear it. Did Lord Beddington take a swing at the wife? Sure, I'm as wise as you. And anyway, they were gentry and they wouldn't like this kind of old talk and that's why Liza was so well got with them. She knew how to cover up and yes, you'd turn in the street to look at her. The shoes always well-polished and a shantung coat of Lady Beddington's altered on her. Good material. It saves money in the long run.

Lightning

Jesus of Nazareth, King of the Jews, from a sudden
and unprovided death, deliver us oh lord!

Dante taught Joyce that prayer with a fear of lightning
and dogs that never left him.
My mother went rigid when she heard
the first rolls and we were told
to keep away from the windows, drag Brownie
by the scruff of his neck to the black hole
where he'd set up a werewolf howling background
to her banshee moan –
Stay away in the name of god from the windows.
The story again of the uncle who died with a greyhound
between his knees – *struck because dogs attract electricity* –
something in their hair.
I felt bad for Brownie in among the coats
and rubbery wellingtons,
the glassy minks giving him the bad eye.
I crawled carefully along the floor to get my book
and a candle as she cried, *Quench all electricity!*
and Brownie howled as if he was being buried alive,
facing a slow suffocating death
as unwinking and uncaring
as a glass eye.

The Reckoning

for Seeta Indrani

For the Jews the Cossacks are always coming
— LINDA PASTAN

For my mother, it was the Bailiff.
I imagined him looking like Mrs Callaghan's
boyfriend who wore a cowboy hat
and cradled a big brandy on his beige thigh,
or maybe I'm mixing him up with the Sheriff.
My mother was afraid of him too.
The Sheriff was the Head of Taxes,
Mrs Callaghan was the lady accountant.
When she left town, the tax people
came after every one of her clients.
What a fool I was, my mother looked
into the hall mirror, her dark eyes
surveying the fool who'd stayed up late
filling Mrs Callaghan's glass, enthralled
by a woman who could be this
confident with everyone's money.
My brother-in-law did the accounts
after that, his curly hard-working head
bent over yards of white tape.
He wanted them to balance
but *how could they?* cried my mother.
We were openly and secretly eating
our way through the shop, inviting the cats
to join us in a big bonanza
of Rancheros, Aztecs and Coke.
We promised to tighten our belts,

would even have liked to lose weight
but soon it was Consulate cigarettes,
Huzzar Vodka, gallons of Maxwell House.
Fear of the Bailiff stayed with me though –
something in the blood because it couldn't be
the history book photos, there were
no cowboy hats in those pictures,
no affable Mrs Callaghan, no boyfriend
raising his ballooning brandy glass –
just black-shawled women, barefoot
children, RIC men with fixed bayonets,
the battering ram.

Known to the Guards

for David Schiff

A guard took my name once
outside the Burnfort school.
His largeness poured tight
into his navy blue uniform
he stood over me and
wrote my name in his notebook.
He said I had a guilty face
when no one owned up
to creating the hullabaloo
outside the post office.
In the nights that followed
when men ran out of the pub
before a raid, I watched the red stars
of their cigarettes darting
like tiny devils in the dark.
Sick to the pit of my stomach,
as hunted as a Hitchcockian character
haunted by the miscarriage of justice
and how that Guard chastised me
standing with his great back to the green
post office in a grey wind.
From now on, he said
with his pan loaf-sized foot poised
on the pedal of his Honda 50,
the Garda Síochána were on to me.

The Traveller

She came alone on foot
and straight away they noticed
she was a rebel; before punk,
before rap she had streaked hair
orange and black
and a loud transistor radio
that blared through the village
that hot day, drowning the sound
of the insects in the grass.
She didn't say ma'am to anyone,
she said, *I don't want your fucking*
ould clothes or your ould fucking
soft apples. She said she wanted money
and she went to every house
repeating her request, kicking foxgloves,
rejecting everything else that was offered.
And no one produced money, only
everyone said that the world had gone mad
and it was only now they realised
weren't the old tinkers lovely
and quiet compared to the cut
of that big one with her transistor
radio bawling under her arm like
a terrible fuck-you voice from the future.
The last place she called was Mikey Dorgan's.
He gave her a half dozen eggs
out of the goodness of his heart
not realizing that she meant business.

It was only when she'd left
he found that she'd pelted the six of them
and they were running in yellow streams
down the back of his gable wall.

Elvis is Dying

Well you may run on for a long time
Run on for a long time,
Run on for a long time
Let me tell you God Almighty's gonna cut you down

This Dalston winter morning, I can stop time
put down the biography
look out at the back garden where
the frost powders the vine twigs –
it's 35 degrees in Memphis, he hasn't gone
to the bathroom yet. I take a look out
the front through frost-blackened
fuchsia – Balls Pond Road,
the woman in full adidas, the man in the truck tapping
the steering wheel, the seagull big as a cat.
When I pick up the book again
he's walking into the big red bathroom
with the black toilet, the chair in the shower. Ginger
sleeps through the Memphis heat, she will put on her make-up
before she checks on him, to the outrage of the eternal millions
crowding round the windows of Graceland
searching YouTube for his dappled shadow
flitting through that antebellum mansion. Behind
my grille of black twigs, I turn the page,
he's down in his face in his own vomit
and I remember his namesake,
that traveller from Cork, Elvis O'Donnell.
Strange to think, he died in a ditch the very same way.

The Shining Steed

'Is it about a bicycle?'
 — FLANN O'BRIEN, *The Third Policeman*

When he led me into the kitchen with my eyes closed,
I was no longer mystified.
Wrapping couldn't hide
that distinctive shape, two wheels, a saddle
and a basket reminding me of nosy Fifi
hanging out of that older basket as I tore
through Burnfort on Ber's bicycle –
she called it her shining steed.
Never occurred to me to want my own
after the shock at seventeen,
falling off Foxy John's hired bicycle,
five stitches on my chin in Dingle hospital
and the priest asking Ber what were two girls
doing out so early in the morning.
I cycled twice since: in traffic-free
Rottnest Island where small marsupial
quokkas hopped, and Inishmore,
also quiet except for the odd sad donkey
with his head over a gate. At forty seven,
I wobble off around the side roads of Mistley,
from time to time meeting a little girl on a pink
bicycle, her tongue out and silver streamers
hanging from her handlebars. Like me, she's intent
on getting in the practice. They say
you never forget and it is true. I'm whizzing
back to the house now, ringing my bell, the sun
glinting on my blue and white wheels.

Getting off, I pat the saddle, wave
to the pink and silver girl as she labours by,
as if she's someone I've been missing
all these years.

Substitute

I think I could turn and live with animals
— WALT WHITMAN

She's talking about when she was a single mother. Like this is some calamity. I'm drifting because I've heard it before and then I have a sense of something unpleasant coming, there's something about not being able to get a man and then she's pointing at me, *Martina will understand me here, I got a cat instead.* I sit there, dumb as an animal thinking about how the four-legged ones don't point at you like that and I think of the Mater Hospital when I was twenty-four, just married and the doctor's breath so wine-rich every morning I just suffocated standing there, passing the cassettes. He said my rescue of the kittens born overnight in the warm cardboard X-ray files was *simple child substitution* and then I think of my father who had the full set of everything, a wife, six daughters and four sons, all at the same time but he is running, mad to get past us, running to the back door, running down the old cracked path as they stream out from every shed and hole in the hedge, from the fir trees and the galvanized roof tops and the warm felted boiler house, ginger, white, black, grey, fawn, their blended colours like a river of spices, spilling along the ground: Hamlet, Rolo, Tickles, Sputnik, Pompeius, Lunar and Gemini, Nuptials, Wardie, Mr 1972, Bimbo and he is shouting into the blue and white puffy Burnfort sky, like I shout now every time I return – *I'm back, I'm back.*

Happy Meat

to Dennis Morton

When you stand in line at the butcher's
listening to the meat slicer's whine,
are you sure?
Has he laid his pink snout on your knee
and assured you that he loves captivity
that he knows nothing of his fate on the block
or in the brine or that if he *does* know
he has complete faith in the farmer's judgement
to kill him at a convenient time
so that when you see him in the future
whether on soft white bread
or stainless steel tine, you can be assured
he went to his death, smiling to the last rind?

Dead Souls

Who thinks it's nice to think of them
smiling down on us?
If they are looking down
they could be frowning or
crying or worse. I pull the Black-
watch tartan rug closer,
sip strong hot black coffee
sink into a soft white banana
and peanut butter sandwich.
Donny, a bundled roll
of white and ginger stripes
groans in his sleep beside me.
Last night, a smiling corpse entered
my dream and hugged me.
I didn't like it all.
Let the dead smile at themselves.

Toasted Cheese

for Fahima Sahabdeen

*'Truly man is the king of beasts, for his brutality exceeds
them. We live by the death of others. We are burial places
. . . Endless numbers of these animals shall have their little
children taken from them, ripped open, and barbarously
slaughtered.*
— LEONARDO DA VINCI, *Notebooks*

Cheese digests all but itself. Mighty cheese.
— *Have you a cheese sandwich?*
— *Yes sir.*
— JAMES JOYCE, *Ulysses*

Toasted cheese featured in one of my earliest picture books –
Granddad on the mountain toasting a slice on the end
of a long fork in an abridged edition of *Heidi*.
Daddy brought home strange lumps of leftover
rubbery stuff for the cats although they seemed
to prefer Cadbury's milk chocolate. I never stopped
to think where the never-ending stream of milk came from –
milk and whey was and is in everything
and especially at Rathduff Cheese factory –
stories of workers falling into outsize vats
like the giant saucepans of fairy tales,
these vats couldn't possibly be filled by the work
of homely milkmaids on three-legged stools.
The cruel river of milk came from elsewhere, like babies
and the queer dreams caused by eating cheese.

I'm thinking of toasted Emmenthal sandwiches –
the holey cheese reminiscent of cute mice in cartoons –

while reading Joyce's Lestragonians with whole-body
    prickling horror
and still envying broken-hearted Bloom
his Gorgonzola and Burgundy,
sitting up at the polished counter in Byrne's.
Take away that. Lubricate. A nice salad, cool as a cucumber.
Tom Kernan can dress. And Costcutters might sell Stilton.
Better to get it all over in one go,
stay up late tonight, for once and for all
eating everything on The Cheese Board.

But *meh*, Bloom said, *wretched brutes waiting at the cattle*
    market,
Staggering Bob – veal from a butchered tottering day-old
    calf.
To glug down his milk, one must believe his mother
    doesn't care.
The cows are waiting to be *pole-axed. Moo. Poor trembling*
    calves.
The Cotswolds, Easter 1999. Liadain got to milk
Buttercup, the single Jersey cow on a sheep farm
full of double-jointed jumping lambs, pure Eden until
we discovered Billy the calf with the chocolate curls locked
away in the dark. 'His mother's milk is too rich for him,'
the farmer was smiling at the soft city slickers. He hoped
for another Gulf War, he said war was good for the farmers,
it was evening when he said that and the sun
seemed to be shooting into the earth as he spoke.

And Billy cried as Buttercup lowed and looked picturesque
in the dusk like a romantic wrapper on a bar
of Swiss chocolate. Or one of those Anchor cows getting
    ready

to play football on a TV ad. And I can't stand any of it.
Packets of M&S sirloin
wrapped with pictures of dappled meadows and photos
of Honest John farmers. Bloom said it. We're all savages,
bad savages. If you can imagine cows
frolicking with footballs, then you must imagine their pain.
If the rich want to slobber in cruelty, don't make up stories
of happy *foie gras*, Fortnum and Mason.
Grandmother Cotter and the servants laughed indulgently
when Daddy cried for his calf going to market.
'Like a pure spoilt fool over animals all his life,' Mammy said.
Uncle Tommy was a proper man. 'And don't forget no one
      loved
horses more.' Tommy bred greyhounds for coursing,
maintained that to see a cat relaxing in a yard
was a sign the dogs were 'pure useless'.

It is tiring and painful, easier to let it go.
Like when the Brits accused the Boers of using dumdum bullets
which they invented themselves for India, the Boers said
they only used them on the blacks or the elephants
and everyone said okay then . . .
White missionary too salty, mutters Bloom
the outcast, ruminating on cannibals. *Like pickled pork.*
Expect the chief consumes the parts of honour. Cauls, mouldy tripes,
windpipes, faked and minced up. With regards
to the exploitation of cows, surely not, my sister
said in the old patronising voice,
Bubble and squeak. Butchers' buckets wobble lights.
Give us that brisket off the hook. Plup. Surely not, they said
when the Jews were melted down for lampshades
and soap. *Rawhead and bloody bones. Flayed glass-eyed sheep hung*
from their haunches, sheepsnouts bloodypapered snivelling nosejam

on sawdust. Top and lashers going out and still I'm heading
for the door, ripping up the zip of my parka,
stopping to tie my shoelaces tight when

'A minute on the lips, forever on the hips,' says
another disembodied voice from the '70s.
I go out into the crisp-leaved October night, not seeing
the amber-glowing copper beech on Balls Pond Road
but windowless artificially-lit factory-farm sheds, hiding
in the dark countryside. *Peace and war depend*
on some fellow's digestion. Religions.
Christmas turkeys and geese. Slaughter of innocents.
Eat, drink and be merry. Then casual wards full after.
Heads bandaged.

Kneel for a while with the fruit jellies,
peering at the tiny print – it's gelatin in every bag and
the E120 in Skittles comes from the Brazilian cochineal
        insects
boiled alive. 70,000 make one pound of *natural* cochineal
        stain
and the sweets are still seduction red.
Am I pure spoilt too like Daddy?
What about big Brazilian families with mouths to feed?
Mouths, mouths, and worst of all, *the hungry famished gull*
of my own mouth now. I buy four Mr Tom
Turkish peanut brittle bars, eat them all in one go,
still thinking of Bloom and his Gorgonzola.
Splintering Mr Tom between my teeth,
I try not to think of other nights of temptation
streaming out ahead of me as I watch *Taking*
Root, a documentary about Wangari Maathai
and her Kenyan women, getting over 'Colinisation',

planting trees. Later, I dream that I've joined the *Mau Mau*,
wake late in a room full of sun with hungry cats
poking at me. One more day,
a murderer reprieved.

The Dawning of the Day

after Dream Endings *by Roisin Tierney*

The first time I drew back
the curtain in this newly bought Dalston wreck,
I heard the clopping of hooves
and there it went – a glass coach with four
black horses and plumes – the corpse, the casket,
the coachman wearing a high hat.
I didn't know about East End funeral carriages,
then they became a regular sight, disappearing
into Our Lady and St Joseph's Catholic churchyard
with their *Mum* and *Dad* wreaths or once a piper
in a plum velvet cloak stopping traffic
as he played *The Dawning of the Day.*
But the shiver still comes back
when I pick up Roisin's *Dream Horses*
and at the same time hear
the hooves on the stone outside. Someone
is *getting the feathers* again – makes me stand
still at the old floor-length windows that
wouldn't pass *Health and Safety* now. The past
is a heavy breath on Balls Pond Road –
the endless vein of oyster shells in the earth,
the ancient wind-up window shutters
coming up on a pulley.
The fear of being buried alive
inclines me towards cremation
and the garden would be the right place

for a scattering, along with Marcel, Eileen
Murphy and Alice's kittens. Fitting when I
have worked so hard to fertilize
that piece of the ground. It's a comfort
and a horror every time I hear the coach clatter.

On the Border

for Joanne and Tony

Balls Pond Road has the cream
of sunsets. Rubbish, boarded-up
squatted buildings, heavy traffic that grinds
and grates under the piercing call
of police cars and over it all clouds,
turquoise, salmon, shell and navy.
My eyes search for each landmark of home:
the plane trees, the big copper beech, the almshouses,
and the recording ghost of Jerry O'Neill
landlord at The Duke of Wellington.
He stands on his flat roof
looking out over Hackney to the East,
Islington to the West and I've lived with his words
for weeks. His poetry of London and
the thrust of this poorest of places
in the sixties and seventies
is both a familiar and queer
last glimpse of a disappearing world.
I can't take my eyes off
his empty roof.
When it grows dark, I garden by electric light,
exchanging tulip bulbs for old
oyster shells in the sticky earth
while the traffic like an angry sea
echoes and booms
through the grubby cliffs of our yellow-bricked buildings.
Later, I will scrub my earthy fingernails,
rinse my hair from a jug as I sit

in the cast-iron tub unglamorously bolted to the floor.
The bath trembles when the lorries rumble by,
reminds me that Georgian bricks aren't cemented
so everything keeps shifting.

The Mystery of Shoes

I avert my eyes passing
shoeshops
but the devil
peers out, ruby eyes
illuminating
a window in Venice
filled with expensive colours
of chocolate, donkey, desert.
Mary Magdalene unbuckling
Jesus's dusty sandals,
all those people in the Bible
showing off their toes,
the gleaming shoes
my daughter begged for,
smart as paint,
strapped to her feet,
they made her shy,
so chic she was afraid
that they'd speak to her.

The Price of Shoes

for Jane and Tim

Shoes speak to Liadain,
her bedroom floor carpeted
with pink high heels, rusty soft
moccasins, red strappy peep
toes, papery worn Robin Hood
boots fixed with PVA glue.
There are ghosts too,
the yellow stilettos I refused
to buy when she was twelve.
Her tiny frame
and big smile balanced
on top of those
long lemon tongues . . .
You can't have them because –
the air so scarce and hot
in Tammy's changing room,
it makes me blurt –
they're like something
a prostitute would wear!
The black Doc Martens
are heroic –
they keep her warm and dry.
She could run fast in them.
The last day of school
Hampstead Heath swells
with drunken teenagers,
and one shiny tobacco-coloured
brogue is lost in the hawthorn.

But I don't share her grief.
I feel relief
as if the shoe is a coin
paid to the wild
for her safe return.

I want to be like Frank O'Hara

but I've never leaned
on a club doorway listening
to Billie Holiday. Most of my time
in this city I've been a mother and I know
I've spent too much time in Sainsbury's
Dalston branch even if it does
have its own inimitable vibe
and a huge range of root vegetables.
My own roots sink deep in the garden and
I can't bear to leave
in case I miss a single bloom
or one of those odd powder-blue
butterflies passing through
on its way to Hackney Marshes.
I swing in the hammock to the echo
of police sirens, but I've never
leaned on a club doorway, my poems
in my pocket like Frank. My books
are stuffed with shopping lists
and I can't believe that's Frank.
Although once at 11 a.m. looking
for the new GP surgery in Green Lanes,
I stuck my head in the doorway
of a Turkish men's club and they scattered
from their chess like leaves.
I felt a bit dangerous then, like Elvis in '56.
I think Frank would have liked it,
the way one brave man approached me slowly,
his hands out in front as if
he was about to catch something.

Valentine

When they were very young, he forgot but he said that he didn't believe in it anyway, it was gross commercialism. Money for stationers and flower shops, verses full of empty formulas. Even talking about it enraged him, as he was enraged now, years later. He'd never said that, she was his dearest valentine. Hadn't he told everyone he was bringing her away for the weekend to a *Country House Hotel*? Of course they could afford it. Wasn't it his right to do it? Wasn't he the man who loved her too much? The woman she thought was her friend, confirmed, yes, everyone at the company knew about it. It would cost thousands, shrieked the friend, sounding a bit enraged herself. Afterwards, she could only remember the beginning, arriving late at night, the sky full of expensive stars, the gravel spitting underfoot as liveried servants respectfully carried in their daughter's twenty-seven soft toys and the end in the leafy foyer, surrounded by the same teddies, dogs, cats and rabbits, waiting to check out, he was beside her, his hands shaking, asking her to pay with her own credit card.

Kept Back

Prayer, the last refuge of the scoundrel
— LISA SIMPSON

Even Bart Simpson felt the shame,
yellow and unreal as he was and
everything distracted him but especially
the snowstorm that God sent – he slumped
slogging over a book while everyone
in Springfield linked arms in a circle,
singing *A Winter Wonderland*.
But I was good at reading. I'd gone
through the library and back, it was all
inside me, how the Japanese houses
were made of paper in case of
earthquake and Eskimos lived
in igloos made of bricks of solid ice
and the length of a boa constrictor
was as long as six boys with American
crew cuts, wearing turned-up jeans on
six bicycles. The prayers were
only an afterthought – didn't we say them
every day until we were sick of them?
The colours of the Ladybird fairy tales scorched
on my brain, Cinderella's three dresses, blue
and pink and gold and roses, and the Elves
and the Shoemaker, blue and green and pink
with gold boots and the Ugly Duckling.

I didn't hear

that it was my mother's decision
until years later when someone said
Mrs McCarthy didn't speak to her for a week.

My mother who revered teachers,
crossing words over this one?
She, who told them not to spare the rod?
All I knew then was what I heard,
the others stumbling over
their Acts of Faith, Hope and Charity –
I was so sure that I knew the Acts
but the teacher's finger pointed straight.
No First Holy Communion for me.
I would never be sure again.
Even Bart managed to woo Miss Krabappel
into giving him a D minus in the end
and he passed into fifth grade.
But I was kept back
outside the ring of First Holy Communion dresses
that went round and round,
white and crisp as a Winter Wonderland.

Oh Bart

Your yellow legs dance in your shorts back and forth, your yellow crowned head at the top of the classroom, winging it with *Treasure Island* under your arm – you haven't read it and you're bluffing and Ms Krabappel's yellow gaze, her upside-down cup of a jaw is unimpressed, fully irritated. We were in a semi-circle, I had my book with Billy Bones and the whole exciting caboodle going on, Blind Pugh and the Black Spot (oh Bart, you missed this) hidden behind my Irish book so when the Master said, *Dun do leabhair, shut the books* – like magic, there was a semi-circle of children with folded hands, ready to be examined, closed textbooks at their feet as they'd been taught and me, like a parody of myself and my bad dreamy reputation sticking out in the middle – my head still stuck between the big covers of the *leabhar* that hid the cover of *Treasure Island*, unaware of the hurricane of spit and hands hurtling towards my head and I still feel it, the black and white shock, back and forth, back and forth, my head in his hands like a ball and when it was over and I raised the latch, stumbling through Burnfort like Blind Pugh tapping along the road, like Long John Silver crawling in the sand without his crutch, like Scratchy, electric sparks circling my head, down the road to her Erin Oxtail soup. She, who told him, *don't spare the rod*, who supported his regime so much that he loved her and they teased me because he used her name for sums. *If Mrs Cotter had seven apples in a bag and she had eight bags and sold two, how many apples, how many would she have? Come on, come on, seven multiplied by eight, what would Mrs Cotter get if she takes away two, what would she get if she took it away?* And *Mrs Cotter*, taken aback by my red and white bruised ball of a head, kept me at home, without a message or an excuse to her admirer, all afternoon.

Putting it On

In the convent secondary school
Sister Benedicta – also known as *Big Ben* –
said I was *putting it on. Acting.*
I didn't know what she was talking about
until copper-haired, brown-eyed Dolores
stood up for me. *She can't help it, Sister,* Dolores said
but Dolores wasn't listened to either when she
tried to explain that I'd learned to stand like that
in National School.
I'd carried it over, unconscious of how
annoying it was for the nuns,
me with my one hand clutching the desk,
one bottle-green stockinged leg braced against
the iron rung underneath, the other
stuck out in front, ready to run.

The Game

The Master himself. A horrible coloured cartoon.
White collar, conservative golden-brown tie,
Brillo-stiff grey hair standing on his head.
The lines folding down his cheeks,
tongue out at the side of his mouth,
his Parker pen sliding up and down
the yellow slabs of teeth, the lime-cordial eyes
darkened with swelling pupils.
His Excitement. The sight of him bent over,
his brown trousers stretched tight through the slit
in his hound's-tooth jacket. Grunting. The children
in front of him dodging back and forth.
Him panting, laughing, waving the whippy ash stick
aiming straight for the tips of their pink-skinned fingers.

The Slap

In the insanity of that room with its dirty mushroom-
coloured walls, when he unrolled the rattling blank map,
cranking himself up as he watched
our blind-mole fingers trying to trace the path
of the *Broad Majestic Shannon* or the boundaries
of the *Rebel County of Cork*. In that one half of a two-
roomed schoolhouse his tall desk creaked
as he leaned over it, his green eyes burning,
his legs in their paper-sharp creased trousers
flying up behind in a dance. We watched
Ronan Shea's six-year-old head
put into a motor-cycle helmet,
the crown of it over his face
or Ray Twomey kicked in the stomach
with a balletic brightly polished shoe. But when it came
to slaps, he never held our hands, we were allowed
to try and move our palms to save our fingers.
It was The Game and you had to have Nerve
but we were small and frightened
and the day he held Bernardine Logan by her
delicate-boned sensitive-redhead's wrist,
a tremor went through us, the captive audience.
I see his spittle-face of triumphalism
thrust up against her titanium
white features, after she tried to stand up to him,
and the turntable of my stomach is unstoppable now
although it is years since she died
and he's long rotten.

The Packing

It was a wad of cardboard, paper, cloth
or even a light board roughly
the size of the palm kept up the sleeve.
Everyone had one. But the boys were
the best at developing the technique.
Come up here to me, Sean Ó Murchú, was
the invitation to a dance and the recipient
would start pulling the sleeve down
and if he was a big boy, there was a kind
of smirking flexing movement which echoed
the grinning Master. *Out with the lámh,*
hold out your hand and the trick was while
the Master was aiming for the fingers
the pupil moved the hand forward
the stick waved through the air and
the blow fell on the packing.
The Master always gave up quickly when
the boys were skilled and grinning themselves
and the stick hit the packing with a whack.
Besides he had many losers to compensate
for the martially confident. He loved
to prove what he thought of as *pure stupidity* –
when Sean put stones up his sleeve
they thudded onto the floorboards one by one,
and the Master was counting in Irish,
A haon, a dó, a trí,
a ceathair, shouting happily
fool, bostoon, pillaloo now, Mr Ó Murchú!

The Prompt

Was he thinking aloud or trying
to help? If we had to stand up to spell
a word *as Gaeilge*, he croaked along with us
and that was all we had to go on with –
tossed every day
on the storm of sounds, the unintelligible language
that must have been beaten *out* of children
on the same spot a hundred years before,
a language filled now with pain and spittle
and because he stuttered
in between the letters, his 'uh' and 'eh' and 'ah'
could be taken for the wrong vowel,
the signal for him to dash
to the drawer for his stick.
We rocked in front of him, our ears
cocked to his tobacco breath,
another game of bluff.

Good Friday

With no food to look forward to
and the strangely imprecise
instructions – two *small* meals so that
whatever amount I had of the stuff
of my chief comfort, I was bound
to feel it was too much
and with Jesus tortured and nailed to the cross
all day, how could anyone enjoy herself?
The whole church decked in black
and two forced visits for a closer look at the situation.
Father Riordan, so blonde in his black vestments,
the altar boys with their black skirts
following the Stations of the Cross
and the whole of Burnfort bobbing up
and down on one knee as the priest
paused to contemplate each piercing picture.
Then the shock every year, when local men
sprang into startling thespians, quiet men
who bought Major cigarettes, Cadbury's
and cans of Coke in the shop,
crying out of the congregation in the voices of Peter
and Jesus and all the apostles during
the reading of the Passion, hurt and betrayed,
cowardly and cruel –
my stomach crying for food
on the day we all prayed
for the souls of perfidious Jews.

Supervised Study

Eugie gets off her high chair
at the top of the study and paces
between our desks, Sister Mary
Eugenius has the bluest eyes and
she walks like a man, like she's never
cared for her own good looks.
She puts the fear of God
in the girls yet she likes me, thinks
I'm good at French. Her subject.
Four brown-papered textbooks
are carefully arranged in what I call a *quad*
over Mario Puzo's *The Godfather*.
I jolt when she pauses by my desk,
attracted by *French Verbs*
ostentatiously displayed on the left.
On top, another textbook, *Maupassant*.

Once, Guy was another secret read,
resting on my knees under the desk
with one eye on the Master. At ten,
the weirder the story, the better
I liked it but now I've moved on
to the Sicilians.
                  Eugie groans with delight
as she plucks Maupassant from the desk,
Quelle histoire? Ah, Vendetta –
très intéressant! I blush, it must
have passed for shyness,
The Godfather is nakedly displayed

on my desk but she does not see it.
Eugie's glad, she tells me, to see
I'm finally settling down
making full use of my God-given ability.

Anatomy Lesson

I've still got my *head in the books*
sucking the clandestine comforts.
I'm twenty and Professor Coakley
jerks his knee like a whip of rope
demonstrating muscle movement
at the top of the class. It's *Tess*
this time on my desk in another *quad*
– *Kitty Clark's Positioning* and others.
Thomas Hardy is morbid enough
for me all right and when the girls sit
forward, I know I'm missing something
interesting about muscles or is it tendons?
I'm sure now that I'm *doomed* to be always holding
the wrong book. The pretty Opus Dei celibate
struggles excitedly through the door
with the rattling skeleton, *Oh Professor Coakley!*
She is called a Numerary, there are rumours
she wears a spiked chain
around her thigh. On top, she is definitely wearing
a desert-coloured Prada sweater, her hair
cut in a perfectly symmetrical shining
brown cap, her face deeply red
before the distinguished Professor.
I hate the way the other girls
look at her, smile and exchange looks.

Flowers in the Attic

I hate Dublin and the radiography lectures
and the X-ray department even more,
they laugh at my Cork accent and one
of them said *Aids is a North Side disease.*
I don't want to be here with the snobby girls
with the Donnybrook accents or the registrar
who has nicknamed me *Cork* even though
he is kind. The girl who loves sailing
asks every single one of us what
our fathers do – owning a pub
sounds like something dirty now.
Alone for a moment, I crawl into the shower
with *Flowers in the Attic* and a cinema-sized
bag of Maltesers. Minutes later, Sister
Patricia taps on the door. She smiles
at her fellow Corkonian. I know she cycles
the underground corridors of St. Vincent's
in the dark evenings, her white veil flying.
I know she knows a fellow oddball.
Now, Tina.
I hide my trashy book behind my back.
*When you've wiped your face, you'll
have to come back to Nuclear Physics.
The Siemens engineer's been in there
for the last five minutes.* I'm nearly twenty-one,
scared I'm pregnant,
no qualifications, no hope yet,
mournfully following her white habit.

That's Entertainment

My mother describes the emigration:
Expensive full fares for the whole family
when we could have all gone for ten pounds
on the Australian government. The fools
we were and Nuala and Mary getting up
non-stop to sing and Mary entertaining
the whole ship for weeks with talk. I think
of my mother's mantra, *For God's sake,*
take your head out of the books and talk
to the customers. Ber tells me how
she remembers Tricia in a rage
when I wouldn't *hop to it*
despite the funeral crowd pouring
down the road, a black mass
of relentless figures, hurrying to our door.
How Tricia flung *Vanity Fair* across the red
and white and blue tiled floor and the other
book lover, Pats Curtain, noticed me,
the way I ran after the book *to mind it first*
before I attended to the customers.
He said that I carefully marked my page.

London Irish

for Marcella Riordan

If I could sing and play the piano
I would like to sit down to thump out
that profound ballad Finnegan's Wake.
Welt the flure your trotters shake – if you sing that
line often enough to yourself
you get a bit of handle
on Joyce's big shake-up of the English
language. No harm at all to feel around
in the dark of your head and see what
comes out. Piling up chickpea flour
at the Madina Store, Mohanlal reaches
out with a lollipop
for Liadain and calls her *baby*
and we laugh even though I know
he knows that's what she is to me
– how did Liadain become twenty?
As we hurry to the vet with ginger Donny
in his comfy leopard-print bag bought online
under the banner – *Live the cappuccino*
life-style! – an Irish wino catches up with
us at the lights. We all stand together
at Dalston Junction and he brandishes
his can like a diviner:
ha ha dee, has the ould fella
deserted ye for William Hill,
is he down below in the pub?
he knows he's spot on
we're on our own
and we don't have to say anything

only laugh again
as the lights change
and we rush on with Donny roaring.
The man twirls like a leaf stuck
to the lamppost, calling after us
that he sees the *Irish* in our faces.

The Green Storybook

for Fiona

Today, the first edition – 1947 – with fine
cross-hatched illustrations arrives from eBay,
in a cellophane-covered never-before-seen
dust wrapper. The apple-coloured
jacket was long gone by the time
The Green Storybook fell into my chubby hands
in the sixties. I taught myself to read
from that book, Enid Blyton's distinctive
script running across the darker green cloth cover.
I would look for her again and again,
the *Secret Garden* door,
that first Royal Flush, the miracle
of the black marks straightening themselves
out into sense across the page,
saying this way, this way
you'll escape.

Also by Martina Evans from Anvil

ๅๅ๐

All Alcoholics Are Charmers

The poems are little dramas and monologues that go straight
to the grudges, disappointments, root-confusions and hang-
ups, showing the depths in trivial things and the trivial in the
deep . . . a pleasure to read and recommend.

HERBERT LOMAS in *Ambit*

Can Dentists Be Trusted?

. . . funny yet disturbingly precise accounts of her parents, their
sweet shop, recalcitrant cats, school and the monologues of
Catholic mothers: '. . . and now Father Tim is all over the
tabloids'. These look like easy, anecdotal poems but they bite.

ALAN BROWNJOHN in *The Sunday Times*

Facing the Public

Martina Evans's poems are a miracle, for the way they
combine total clarity with profundity: the way the apparently
innocent and observant humour of their narrative surface
covers a compassion and understanding that are often heart-
breaking and heartbroken.

BERNARD O'DONOGHUE

Petrol

In *Petrol*, Martina Evans has shaped rural Irish girlhood into an
extended prose poem. . . . *Petrol* deals in unacceptable desires,
semi-disgusting longings, yearning, lust and loss. It is a marvel-
lous poem of youth, insightfully evoking a vanished Ireland
and bringing the past to palpitating life.

CHLOE STOPA-HUNT in *Poetry Review*